LOBSTER

40 DELICIOUS RECIPES FOR CANADA'S EAST COAST DELICACY

ELAINE ELLIOT & VIRGINIA LEE

FORMAC PUBLISHING COMPANY LIMITED

Formac Publishing Company Limited recognizes the support of the Province of Nova Scotia through the Department of Communities, Culture and Heritage. We are pleased to work in partnership with the Culture Division to develop and promote our culture resources for all Nova Scotians. We acknowledge the financial support of the Government of Canada through the Canada Book Fund for our publishing activities. We acknowledge the support of the Canada Council for the Arts which last year invested $24.3 million in writing and publishing throughout Canada.

Design by Meghan Collins

Library and Archives Canada Cataloguing in Publication
Elliot, Elaine, 1939-, author
    Lobster : 40 delicious recipes for Canada's east coast delicacy / Elaine Elliot and Virginia Lee.

Includes index.
ISBN 978-1-4595-0313-7 (bound)

    1. Cooking (Lobsters). 2. Cooking (Shellfish). 3. Cooking--Maritime Provinces. 4. Cookbooks. I. Lee, Virginia, 1947-, author II. Title. III. Title: Lobster : forty delicious recipes for Canada's east coast delicacy.

TX754.L63E445 2014   641.6'95   C2014-902898-9

Formac Publishing Company Limited
5502 Atlantic Street
Halifax, Nova Scotia, Canada
B3H 1G4
www.formac.ca

Printed and bound in Canada.

CONTENTS

INTRODUCTION 5

STARTERS 15

SOUPS 33

LUNCH 47

MAINS 67

INDEX 92

PHOTO CREDITS 95

INTRODUCTION

It's hard to believe that lobster hasn't always been regarded as the gourmet food it is today. Just a few decades ago, for many fishermen's families in Atlantic Canada, eating lobster was a sign of poverty — it meant that you were too poor to buy bologna. Now, thanks to gourmet styles and a strong interest in seafood, lobster appears on menus across the country and is served at community-run lobster suppers throughout the Maritime provinces. This book of recipes from chefs across Canada demonstrates how versatile lobster and other popular shellfish can be in appetizers, soups, lunches and entrées.

Lobsters (*Homarus americanus*) are caught from the ocean floor. Studies have shown that early juveniles prefer rocky, cobbled bottoms, while adults are generally regarded as relatively solitary, highly migratory animals. A lobster grows by moulting, or shedding, its shell; this occurs about twenty-five times during the first five years of life, increasing the lobster's size 20 per cent each time. After a moult, which usually takes place in the summer, the lobster is soft-shelled and filled with the seawater it has absorbed in the process. Up to two months passes before the water is replaced by new lobster flesh. As the shell hardens in the cold waters of the North Atlantic, the lobster acquires a denser, fuller feel, giving the meat the texture and taste that consumers prefer. It takes five years for a lobster to grow to one pound and up to twenty years for it to reach four pounds.

⚓

Lobsters are most abundant off the coasts of Nova Scotia, New Brunswick and Prince Edward Island, and in the Gulf of St. Lawrence and the Gulf of Maine. They're harvested and processed in the three Maritime provinces, Newfoundland and Quebec. Landings peak twice a year, once from April to June, when the spring season opens, and again in December, after the winter fishery starts in southwestern Nova Scotia.

Atlantic Canada's staggered fishing seasons are designed to protect the stock, and the waters are divided into forty-one lobster fishing areas, each with its own season varying in length from eight weeks to eight months. This seasonal effort is complemented by new and innovative holding and processing techniques. Most of the lobster fishery takes place fairly close to shore, but a few vessels fish the deep basins and outer banks off southwestern Nova Scotia. Five provinces participate in the catch, with Nova Scotia, New Brunswick and Prince Edward Island accounting for 90 per cent of lobster landings and Quebec and Newfoundland making up the remaining 10 per cent. Currently, there are about 9,000 licensed lobster fishermen, of which nearly 3,000 are in Nova Scotia.

Licensed lobster fishermen — usually a captain and two or three crew members — set their traps from small boats, heading out on the water in the early hours of the morning and staying out for up to twelve hours. The brightly coloured buoys mark the areas where they leave their traps. They return several hours later to haul up the wooden-frame or plastic-coated steel-mesh traps from the sea floor.

In Prince Edward Island, lobster has been the mainstay of the economy since the fishery began in the mid-1870s, although it almost died in its infancy. In the mid-1880s — only ten years after the boom began — over-fishing drove the stocks to dangerously low levels, and the fishery faced ruin. It was saved by a combination of regulation, co-operation and luck.

Commercial canning helped the lobster fishery flourish in all parts of the Maritimes. The first known cannery opened on Prince Edward Island in 1858. Within twenty-five years, thanks to the lobster fishery, the number of Island canneries had risen to more than a hundred, and the lobster fishery accounted for 25 per cent of the province's income. Without canning, the lobster would never have found its way to lucrative markets in Great Britain and the United States, where it was considered a delicacy.

The success and prosperity of the present-day lobster fishery is evident in towns and villages across the Maritimes. It challenges the stereotype of hardscrabble life in a fishing village. Inevitably there has been controversy about the control of licenses, fishing seasons and the number of traps in a given area. In 1999, the New Brunswick community of Burnt Church became a hotbed of tension between native and non-native lobster fishermen. The native fishermen were exercising their treaty right to set lobster traps throughout the year, regardless of the season. During the often violent demonstrations, non-native fishermen destroyed native traps, fish plants, boats and equipment.

A moratorium helped defuse the trouble, and in 2002, the federal government released a report aimed at preventing more conflict. It recommended that all charges stemming from the confrontation be dropped and that Ottawa should compensate the fishermen for their lost traps and boats. It also recommended that native fishermen adhere to the same season as non-natives, meaning they would be banned from fishing lobster in the fall.

⚓

Traditionally, live lobsters are held in pounds — large, fenced areas of the ocean — but recently, huge dry-land holding facilities pioneered in Atlantic Canada have made possible a three-million-pound live inventory of the region's best lobsters. As a result, international buyers can get a year-round supply of the top-quality Canadian crustaceans. Lobster is Canada's most valuable seafood export, contributing as much as $1 billion in export sales each year.

Larger lobsters generally are sold in the fresh, live market where they command top prices, while smaller ones are cooked and either frozen whole or shelled for meat. Most of the lobsters caught in the waters of Nova Scotia, Newfoundland and Quebec go to the live market, which means consumers can select and buy them from tanks in grocery stores, fish markets or directly from fishermen at the wharf.

Clearwater Seafoods, a Nova Scotia company, has become almost synonymous with lobster. In 1976, it started out as a small, local distributor, with two co-owners running the business out of a pickup truck. They quickly developed a strategy and infrastructure for storing lobsters and distributing to markets worldwide. From their company headquarters in Bedford they started shipping planeloads of live lobster to destinations in Europe and the United States. The company has joined forces with the government to ensure the responsible management of lobster stocks. It is also dedicated to putting new and improved technology in place.

In Arichat, Cape Breton, one million lobsters can be found resting in "private apartments," where temperatures are maintained just above the freezing mark. This hi-tech Clearwater facility is designed to store lobsters for long periods of time. Tricked into thinking it's always winter, they don't moult when summer arrives and continue to grow and mature in the safety of their compartment. Sixty people work in the plant, sometimes around the clock. At times, the volume of lobsters arriving in a single day can reach 100,000.

⚓

Sold live, cooked, frozen and canned to consumers in more than fifty-five countries around the world, lobster is one of the exports most closely associated with Canada. Almost every part of a lobster can be used in some culinary way, except for the digestive tract, the antennae and mouth parts. The empty shells can be used in bisques or for lobster au gratin; the green tomalley that fills the cooked body cavity is excellent in spreads, sauces, dips and butters; and the roe — the red, unfertilized eggs — is also very tasty.

Served hot, lobster meat adds richness to casseroles, stir-fries, stuffings, sauces, bisques, omelettes, soufflés, quiches and many other dishes. Cold, it's wonderful in salads, hors d'oeuvres and the famous East Coast lobster roll.

The recipes in this book range from Lobster Potato Salad to Huron County
Lobster Chowder to Barbecued Lobster with Red Pepper and Lime Butter.

Lobster meat is an excellent source of protein, more healthful than
hamburger and nearly fat-free — as long as it's not dipped in drawn butter. It
contains many minerals and vitamins, as well as omega-3 fatty acids, which
help reduce the risk of heart attack.

Traditional lobster suppers are perhaps most popular throughout Prince
Edward Island, although they also are held in many other Atlantic Canadian
communities. At these suppers, which are generally held from early June to
mid-October, a succulent whole, cooked lobster is served in its shell, often
with a side dish of seafood chowder, a freshly baked roll, salad and a dessert,
such as blueberry pie. Diners indulge in the ritual art of extracting cooked
lobster from the shell. This takes some practice and is messy enough to
require a bib and several napkins. After a few attempts, one gets the hang of
using a lobster cracker and a pick to pry and pull out the meat. And after the
first taste, most aficionados never let a summer go by without one communal
lobster supper.

⚓

This book also includes recipes for other favourite Canadian shellfish, including the various species of crab. On the East Coast, the most popular is the Atlantic snow crab (*Chionoecetes opilio*), which is occasionally called spider crab or queen crab. Only the males are harvested because females never exceed the legal minimum size. As with the lobster fishery, the government carefully regulates the number of licenses and fishing seasons. Atlantic snow crab and rock crab (*Cancer irrovatus*) are harvested in the Gulf of St. Lawrence and off Cape Breton Island and Newfoundland, forming a lucrative fishing-and-processing industry.

Most common to the Pacific West Coast is the Dungeness crab (*Cancer magister*) and the King crab (*Paralithodes camtschatica*), the patriarch of the crab family, which is sometimes called the Alaska king crab. Dungeness crabs are found from Alaska to California, and this fishery has an important economic impact on Vancouver Island and its surrounding areas. Crabs are marketed whole, live or cooked. Alternatively, crab meat is sold in cans or frozen packages.

Mussels, clams and scallops are small edible shellfish found in most fish markets. Aquaculture of mussels has been a high-growth industry in the Atlantic region, particularly in Prince Edward Island. Today the province produces more than 80 per cent of the mussel landings in Canada, contributes about $50 million to the provincial economy and employs about 1,500 Islanders.

These bivalves grow on long lines suspended in the water and are harvested in winter and spring when the flesh is in its best form. They're sold live, and the shells can be lightly tapped before cooking to make sure that the mussel closes tightly, indicating that it is alive. It is recommended never to cook and eat any that are not alive, and to discard any that gape open or have broken shells.

Clams, like mussels, are sold live in the shell, or uncooked and shucked in plastic containers. Processed clams are also readily available in cans. The Nova Scotia soft-shell clam (*Mya aremaria*) and the hard-shell quahog (*Mercenaria mercenaria*) are the most prized. On the West Coast, the manila clam (*Tapes pilippinarum*) and the littleneck clam (*Protoaca staminea*) are most frequently harvested in the wild or farmed.

One of the most succulent shellfish species is the sea scallop (*Placopecten magellanicus*), which is found along the eastern North Atlantic, from the northern Gulf of St. Lawrence to northern Newfoundland and Cape Hatteras, North Carolina. The ivory to pinkish-white meat is the adductor muscle that holds the shell together. Since scallops survive for only a short time out of the water, they must be shucked after harvesting and sold fresh or frozen. The term "scallop" shouldn't be confused with the American bay scallop (*Argopecten irradians*), which also is found in Atlantic waters, but is much smaller.

Pacific Coast scallops include spiny scallops (*Chlamys hastate*) and pink scallops (*Chlamys rubida*). Found mainly on the west coast of Vancouver Island and in the Strait of Georgia, these smaller species range in colour from ivory to pinkish-white or pale golden brown. Their texture is similar to sea scallops and their flavour is both sweet and briny. Most scallops are harvested in the wild; however, scientists on both coasts are studying how to farm them through aquaculture.

There are many shrimp species on the market today, and they come in several different sizes and from numerous sources. They are harvested wild and also raised in shrimp farms. Shrimp, also known as prawns, are available fresh, frozen, cooked and raw, as well as shelled, unshelled and canned. They range in size from a tiny salad shrimp to jumbo shrimp and take very little time to cook.

The recipes in this revised edition of *Lobster*, which have been provided by talented chefs from across Canada, are for a wide range of rich and mouthwatering crab, lobster, clam, mussel, shrimp and scallop dishes. Thanks to innovations in delivering fresh shellfish, freezing and canning, they can be prepared throughout the year. While lobster remains the biggest crowd pleaser, all of the dishes featured in this book celebrate the gourmet rewards of the sea.

STARTERS

In our travels we have found talented chefs utilizing the ocean's bounty in a variety of first-course dishes. From succulent Lobster-stuffed Mushroom Caps to Asian-inspired Hoisin Lobster Lettuce Wraps, we are sure you will want to try these creations.

LOBSTER-STUFFED MUSHROOM CAPS

Lobster is a Prince Edward Island specialty and these stuffed mushroom caps are a decadent appetizer suitable for a special occasion.

16 large mushroom caps, stems removed
4 tbsp (60 mL) butter, portioned
2 tbsp (30 mL) all-purpose flour
½ cup (125 mL) heavy cream (35% M.F.)
1 tbsp (15 mL) dry white vermouth
2 tbsp (30 mL) lobster or fish broth
scant pinch of nutmeg
pinch of cayenne pepper
1 tsp (5 mL) paprika
8 oz (225 g) fresh lobster meat, in small pieces
Béarnaise Sauce (recipe follows)
½ cup (125 mL) grated Jarlsberg cheese

Clean mushroom caps. Melt 2 tablespoons (30 mL) butter in a skillet over medium heat and sauté mushrooms until slightly browned and tender. Place mushrooms in a single layer in the bottom of a shallow baking dish. Set aside.

Melt remaining amount of butter in a large saucepan. Whisk in flour and cook until roux is bubbly and slightly browned, about 5 minutes. Stir in cream, vermouth and broth; cook, stirring constantly, until thickened. Season with nutmeg, pepper and paprika. Fold in lobster meat and spoon into mushroom caps. Top each mushroom with a tablespoon of Béarnaise Sauce, sprinkle with grated cheese and broil, 6 inches from the element, until hot and bubbly.

Serves 4 to 6

BÉARNAISE SAUCE

3 egg yolks
1 tsp (5 mL) lemon juice
1½ tsp (7 mL) cider vinegar
½ tsp (2 mL) dried tarragon
½ cup (125 mL) unsalted butter, melted

In a food processor, blend egg yolks, lemon juice, vinegar and tarragon for 10 seconds. Continue to process while slowly adding melted butter in a steady stream. Serve immediately.

LOBSTER-STUFFED TOMATOES

A version of this recipe was shared with us several years ago and we have adapted it to utilize our succulent Nova Scotia lobster and summer's abundant supply of vine-ripened tomatoes. Any large tomato variety will do but for optimum flavour we use heirlooms.

4 large vine-ripened tomatoes
6 oz (185 g) cooked lobster meat, chopped
1 shallot, finely minced
1 clove garlic, finely minced
1 tablespoon finely chopped fresh tarragon leaves
¼ cup (50 mL) butter, softened
salt and pepper
Sweet Pepper Sauce (recipe follows)

Using a sharp knife, remove a sliver off the bottom of each tomato so they will stand in a baking dish. Take a ¼-inch (½-cm) slice off the top of each tomato and scoop out the seeds with a teaspoon, being careful to keep the tomatoes' shape.

Preheat oven to 325°F (160°C). Combine lobster, shallot, garlic, tarragon and butter, season with salt and pepper. Gently stuff tomato shells and cover with tomato top. Bake for 10 to 15 minutes, until heated through. Reserve and keep warm.

SWEET PEPPER SAUCE

1 red and 1 yellow sweet pepper
2 tablespoons olive oil
salt and pepper

Toss the peppers in a bowl with oil, then roast in a 400°F (200°C) oven
for 20 minutes. Place the peppers back in the bowl and cover with plastic
wrap, and let rest until cool. Peel peppers, halve and remove seeds. Using
a blender, purée each pepper separately until smooth. Season with salt and
pepper.

To serve: drizzle a little of each sauce on a plate and top with a warm
stuffed tomato.

Serves 4

CREAM CHEESE LOBSTER CAKES

The sweet lobster flavour and creamy cheese centre of these cakes make a delicious first course. For a luncheon dish or main-course entrée, just add a salad and warm crusty bread.

¼ cup (60 mL) finely chopped red bell pepper
¼ cup (60 mL) finely sliced green onion
¼ cup (60 mL) finely sliced celery
1 tbsp (15 mL) fresh lemon juice
1 tbsp (15 mL) jalapeño hot sauce, or to taste
8 oz (250 g) whipped cream cheese, room temperature
1 cup (250 mL) fine breadcrumbs
½ tsp (2 mL) thyme
½ tsp (2 mL) basil
pinch of salt
pinch of pepper
1 lb (450 g) cooked lobster meat, diced
2–3 tbsp (30–45 mL) butter
Creole Mustard Sauce (recipe follows)
fresh herbs

In a skillet over medium heat, sauté pepper, onion, celery, lemon juice and pepper sauce until the vegetables wilt, about 5 minutes. Remove from heat and stir in whipped cream cheese until combined. Set aside. In a bowl, combine breadcrumbs, thyme, basil, salt and pepper. Set aside.

Cup your hand and place about 2 tbsp (30 mL) of the lobster meat into it. With a blunt knife, spread about 2 tbsp (30 mL) cream cheese mixture over the lobster. Add another 2 tbsp (30 mL) of lobster, press down and form into a ball. Roll the ball in the crumb mixture until well coated. Place the ball on a cutting board and press lightly to form a cake about ¾-inch (2-cm) thick. Repeat process to form 12 lobster cakes.

Heat butter in a skillet over medium-high heat. Add lobster cakes, being careful not to crowd, and sauté until golden on both sides.

To serve: arrange 2 or 3 cakes on each serving plate, drizzle with Creole Mustard Sauce and garnish with fresh herbs.

Serves 4 to 6

CREOLE MUSTARD SAUCE

3 tbsp (45 mL) pepper jelly
¼ cup (60 mL) fresh orange juice
¼ cup (60 mL) Creole mustard

In a small saucepan over low heat, combine pepper jelly, orange juice and mustard; stir until sauce consistency. Serve warm.

Yields ½ cup

WARM ATLANTIC LOBSTER DIP

Easily prepared in advance and popped in the oven just before serving, this dish has become an east coast favourite. It is guaranteed to disappear quickly once your guests arrive!

12 oz (375 g) cooked lobster meat, finely chopped
8 oz (250 g) cream cheese, softened
4 tbsp (60 mL) egg-based mayonnaise
salt and pepper to taste
assorted crackers

In a bowl, blend together lobster, cream cheese and mayonnaise; season with salt and pepper. Turn into a shallow baking dish; cover and refrigerate.

At serving time, preheat oven to 325°F (160°C) and bake for 20 to 30 minutes or until bubbly and lightly browned on top. Serve with assorted crackers.

Yields 2 cups

LOBSTER POUTINE

1 lobster, 1½ lb (500–675 g)
2 shallots, finely minced
½ tsp fennel seeds
2 bay leaves
1 cup (250 mL) white wine
1 cup heavy cream (35% M.F.)
½ tsp (2 mL) paprika
1 tbsp (15 mL) tomato paste
canola oil for deep-frying
8–10 russet potatoes (unpeeled, washed), cut into batonettes
salt and ground pepper
1 lb (450 g) cheese curds
finely chopped chives or green onions, for garnish

In a large pot of boiling salted water, cook the lobster for 4 to 5 minutes. Immediately cool in ice water. Remove meat from the shell and reserve. For the "gravy" gently sauté the shallots, fennel seeds and bay leaves until aromatic but not coloured. Add the wine and reduce slightly. Add in the lobster meat to finish cooking (approximately 1 minute). Remove the lobster meat with a slotted spoon and whisk in the cream, paprika and tomato paste. Reduce by half and remove from heat. (This could be done well in advance.) Add the lobster meat and gently reheat it while you make the fries.

For the fries, heat the oil in a deep fryer or large pot (if at home) to 300°F (150°C). Cook the potatoes in the hot oil for 4 minutes to blanch them. Drain and let sit for a few minutes on a baking sheet to prevent them from sticking. Bring the oil temperature to to 350°F (180°C). Cook the fries 2 to 3 minutes more, until golden and crispy. Drain on paper towels and season with salt and pepper.

To serve, top the fries with the cheese curds and lobster gravy with the lobster meat. Finish by garnishing with fresh chives or green onions.

Serves 4

SHELLFISH WITH YUCATAN FLAVOURS

Laced with spices and natural citrus flavours, this mouthwatering shellfish dish will have you yearning for an exotic southern vacation. This recipe lends itself to preparation in advance; simply assemble and pop in the oven.

3 lbs shellfish of choice (e.g. mussels, clams, shrimp)
8 ounces cooked lobster, chopped
3 garlic cloves, minced
1 jalapeño pepper, seeded and chopped
1 tbsp (15 mL) chili powder
1 tbsp (15 mL) paprika
1 tsp (5 mL) ground cumin
½ tsp (2 mL) oregano
¼ tsp (1 mL) ground cinnamon
¼ tsp (1 mL) ground cloves
2 tbsp (30 mL) beer
juice of 1 lime and 1 orange
2 tbsp (30 mL) olive oil
2 tbsp (30 mL) chopped cilantro
fresh cilantro and orange wedges, for garnish

Rinse shellfish with fresh cold water and drain. Discard any clams or mussels that are cracked or do not close when lightly tapped. Set aside in a large bowl.

Preheat oven to 425°F (220°C). In a blender, combine garlic, jalapeño pepper, dry spices, beer, lime and orange juices and olive oil; purée until smooth. Pour marinade over shellfish, toss to coat and let stand for 5 minutes.

Pour shellfish and marinade into a large shallow roasting pan. Bake, uncovered, stirring once after 10 minutes. Continue baking until mussels and clams have fully opened, about 5 to 10 minutes longer. Discard any shellfish that did not open. Add lobster to pan and heat through.

To serve: Pour onto one large or 6 individual serving dishes; garnish with chopped cilantro and accompany with orange wedges.

Serves 6

PICANT LOBSTER SALAD

Sweet, fresh Atlantic lobster blends well with the fresh lime and cilantro flavours of this interesting salad. You may present the salad on crisp green asparagus, but feel free to serve with other green salads.

12 green asparagus spears
1 lb (450 g) cooked lobster meat, coarsley chopped
4–5 tbsp (60–75 mL) fresh lime juice
2 tbsp (30 mL) extra virgin olive oil
1 tsp (5 mL) crushed pink peppercorns
¼ cup (60 mL) chopped fresh cilantro
1 large avocado, peeled and cubed
salt
cilantro sprigs and lime wedges, as garnish

Trim asparagus and steam until al dente. Drain and rinse under cold water to stop cooking; set aside. Chop lobster meat and set aside.

In a bowl, combine lime juice, olive oil, peppercorns and cilantro; add lobster meat and avocado and stir to combine. Adjust seasoning with salt to taste and marinate for 30 minutes.

To serve: fan three asparagus spears on each of 4 serving plates; place a spoonful of lobster mixture where the stalks meet. Garnish with lime wedges and a sprig of cilantro.

Serves 4

LOBSTER POTATO SALAD

Catch Restaurant, Calgary, AB

At Catch Restaurant, the chef serves this delectable salad garnished with oven-dried strawberries.

2 whole lobsters, 1 lb (500 g) each
8 large strawberries, quartered
¼ cup (60 mL) balsamic vinegar
1 lb (500 g) fingerling or baby potatoes, halved
1 shallot, sliced
1 clove garlic, crushed
2 sprigs fresh thyme
1 bay leaf
½ tsp (2 mL) salt
½ tsp (2 mL) crushed black pepper
olive oil
½ cup (125 mL) mayonnaise
1 tbsp (15 mL) grainy mustard
½ lemon, juiced
chopped chives, as garnish

Cook lobsters in boiling salted water for 10 minutes. Drain and rinse under cold running water. Remove lobster from shell, being careful to keep claws intact. Chop lobster tail meat into 1-inch (3-cm) pieces and refrigerate.

Preheat oven to 250°F (120°C). Toss strawberry quarters with balsamic vinegar and spread on a baking sheet. Bake until dried and slightly wrinkled, about 40 minutes. Cool and reserve.

Place potatoes, shallot, garlic, thyme, bay leaf, salt and pepper in a saucepan and add enough olive oil to cover potatoes. Bring to a slow simmer and cook until potatoes are tender. Cool potatoes in the oil, then drain. Remove bay leaf and thyme sprigs.

While potatoes are cooling, combine mayonnaise, mustard and lemon juice. To serve, toss potatoes with mayonnaise and reserved lobster meat. Divide among four plates and top each salad with a lobster claw. Garnish with strawberries and chopped chives.

Serves 4

HOISIN LOBSTER LETTUCE WRAPS

½ cup flour, all purpose
1 tbsp cornstarch
1 lobster, 1 lb (450 g) raw meat, pieces
¼ cup vegetable or peanut oil
1 tbsp sesame oil
3 cloves garlic, minced
1 tbsp ginger, minced
1 large carrot, finely julienned
2 tbsp soya sauce
½ cup hoisin sauce
1 tbsp Sriracha sauce, optional
2 tbsp sugar
4 tbsp chicken stock
¼ cup roasted cashews, pieces
sesame seeds, toasted
4 green onions, finely chopped
1 head Boston lettuce or iceberg, cleaned
½ English cucumber, peeled and finely diced

Mix together the flour and cornstarch in a bowl. Dust the pieces of lobster in the flour and starch mixture. Add oil to a saute pan or wok and bring to a medium-high heat. Add the lobster and reduce heat to medium, continually turning and stirring the lobster until cooked through (about 3 minutes) and remove with a slotted spoon. Add the garlic, ginger and carrots to the same pan and cook until aromatic. Add the soya sauce, hoisin sauce, Sriracha sauce, sugar and chicken stock, and simmer to reduce slightly. Add back in the lobster and half the cashews to heat.

Pour mixture into a presentation bowl and sprinkle with sesame seeds, green onions, remainder of the cashews and place the bowl in the center of the plate and surround with lettuce cups. Sprinkle diced cucumber all around the plate.

Serves 4 as an appetizer

SOUPS

You can never have too many soup or chowder recipes in your collection, and we are sure you will be intrigued by these unique ones. Bring warmth to your table with earthy Huron County Lobster Chowder or celebrate a warm sunny day with a bowl of chilled Gazpacho with Lobster Claws.

DUNES' SEAFOOD CHOWDER WITH LOBSTER

The Dunes Café, Brackley Beach, PEI

The chef at the Dunes Cafe prepares the fish stock in advance. While we offer the directions for stock, novice cooks can substitute bottled clam juice or stock made with powdered or paste fish bouillon.

4 cups (1 L) Fish Stock (recipe follows)
4 tbsp (60 mL) butter
4 tbsp (60 mL) all-purpose flour
⅛ tsp (½ mL) nutmeg
salt and white pepper to taste
4 large potatoes, peeled and cut in large dice
4 tbsp (60 mL) butter (2nd amount)
½ cup (125 g) chopped onion
½ cup (125 g) chopped celery
1 lb (500 g) lobster meat
3 oz (100 g) salmon fillet, in small chunks
3 oz (100 g) sole or haddock fillet, in small chunks
4 oz (125 g) shrimp, shelled
½ lb (225 g) mussels, steamed and shelled
1 cup (250 mL) heavy cream (35% M.F.)

Place fish stock in a large pot and heat to a simmer. Combine butter and flour to make a paste. Whisk butter mixture into hot stock, bring to a boil and cook 2 minutes, stirring constantly. Season with nutmeg, salt and pepper; set aside.

Cook potato cubes gently in salted water until just tender. Drain and reserve.

Melt second amount of butter in a skillet and sauté onion and celery until soft. Stir in all of the seafood and simmer 3 minutes. Combine seafood and reserved potatoes with thickened fish stock and adjust seasonings, if necessary. Add cream and bring to serving temperature. Do not boil.

Serves 4 to 6

FISH STOCK

6 cups (1½ L) water
1 lb (450 g) fish bones
1 bay leaf
3 whole cloves
1 medium onion, peeled

Place water and fish bones in a large kettle. Stick bay leaf and cloves into onion and add to pot. Bring to a boil, reduce heat and simmer 20 minutes. Strain.

GAZPACHO WITH LOBSTER CLAWS

Serve this Mediterranean style soup during the sunny and hot days of August when vine-ripened tomatoes are at their peak. Remember, the soup is prepared early and chilled for about 12 hours to allow the flavours to blend.

1 medium onion
1 garlic clove
½ English cucumber, pared and seeded
1 green pepper, in chunks
4–5 large vine-ripened tomatoes
½ cup (125 mL) oil
¼ cup (60 mL) vinegar
2 cups (500 mL) water
½ tbsp (8 mL) paprika
1 slice of bread
pinch of caraway seeds
4 whole peppercorns
salt
4 cooked and shelled lobster claws

Combine all ingredients except lobster claws and process in batches in a food processor or blender. Refrigerate 10 to 12 hours. Serve in chilled cups topped with a lobster claw.

Serves 4

LOBSTER SHABU SHABU

5 cups (1¼ L) water
1 small ginger root, peeled and sliced
4 oz (85 g) dried 'kombu' seaweed
6 oz (170 g) tofu, cut into chunks
6 oz (170 g) shiitake mushrooms, stems removed
6 oz (170 g) Enoki mushrooms, stalks removed
1 tbsp soy sauce
1 tbsp sesame oil
1 bunch cilantro, trimmed
1 bunch green onions, cut in 1-inch (2.5-cm) long pieces
16 oz (450 g) raw lobster pieces (meat from 2 lobsters)
Ponzu Sauce, for dipping (recipe follows)

Bring the water with ginger and dried seaweed to a boil and reduce heat. Simmer over a medium heat for 10 minutes. Remove seaweed. Bring the broth back to a boil. Add the tofu, shiitake mushrooms, Enoki, soy sauce, sesame oil, cilantro and green onions. Serve the boiling broth at the table with a platter of artistically arranged lobster. Immediately have your guests cook their lobster by dipping it in the broth with fondue skewers or forks. The lobster can be eaten as is or dipped in a flavourful ponzu type sauce. The remainder of the broth should be served in small soup cups and enjoyed after the all of the lobster has been cooked.

  Chef's Note: It is important that the broth be served as hot as possible, therefore it's recommended to use a very heavy pot like cast iron.

PONZU SAUCE

4 tbsp soy sauce
3 tbsp dashi stock
2 tbsp lemon juice
1 tbsp rice vinegar
2 tsp mirin

Combine all ingredients in a bowl and stir.

Serves 4 to 6

MEDITERRANEAN SEAFOOD STEW

The chef noted that this stew, when served with fresh crusty bread, makes a delicious full-bodied entrée. Plan to prepare the dish in two stages so that the tomato broth can reach its full flavour.

½ tbsp (8 mL) vegetable oil
¼ medium onion, chopped
1 large garlic clove, minced
3 oz (100 g) fresh spinach, chopped
1 tsp (5 mL) fresh coriander (optional)
salt and pepper to taste
7 cups (1½ L) crushed tomatoes
1 tbsp (15 mL) sugar
½ tsp (2 mL) jalapeño pepper, seeded and finely chopped
3 cups (750 mL) fish stock
⅔ cup (150 mL) water
½ tsp (2 mL) crushed fennel seed
1 lb (450 g) fresh mussels, scrubbed and debearded
2 lb (900 g) haddock fillet, bite size pieces
¾ lb (375 g) scallops
¾ lb (375 g) cooked lobster meat, chopped
½ lb (225 g) fresh clam meat
fresh parsley and lemon slices to garnish

In a large stock pot, heat oil over high heat and sauté onion and garlic until softened but not browned. Add spinach, season with coriander, salt and pepper and lower heat. Add tomatoes, sugar, jalapeño peppers and stock; simmer, stirring occasionally, for 30 minutes. Refrigerate broth for up to three days to enhance the flavour.

Reheat tomato broth over low heat. In a large saucepan bring ⅔ cup water and fennel seeds to a boil over medium heat. Add mussels, cover and steam 3 minutes. Add haddock, scallops, lobster and clam meat, bring back to a boil and steam for an additional 2 minutes or until the mussels are open. Remove seafood from poaching liquid and add to tomato broth, discarding any mussels that have not opened.

Serve in shallow soup bowls garnished with fresh parsley and lemon slices.

Serves 6 to 8 generously

SPICY THAI LOBSTER NOODLE SOUP

All Seasons Cafe, Nelson, BC

The red chilies in Thai cooking are hot, but not overpowering. If you want more heat, consider adding a touch of red curry paste to the soup component. Whether you like it hot or hotter, enjoy!

14-oz (398-mL) can coconut cream
1 cup (250 mL) chicken stock
1½ tsp (7 mL) grated ginger root
1 stalk lemongrass, bruised
3 Kaffir lime leaves* (or 1 tsp/5 mL lime zest)
1 tsp (5 mL) fish sauce
1 tsp (5 mL) brown sugar
2 baby bok choy
3 oz (100 g) dried egg noodles
1 tbsp (15 mL) peanut oil
1 lb (450 g) cooked lobster meat, chopped
1 medium red Thai chili, seeded and thinly sliced
1 tbsp (15 mL) fresh lime juice
¼ cup (60 mL) chopped cilantro
lime slices, as garnish

In a saucepan, combine coconut cream, chicken stock, ginger root, lemongrass, lime leaves, fish sauce and brown sugar; bring to a simmer and cook 5 minutes. Strain; return to saucepan and keep warm; do not boil.

Trim bok choy; separate leaves and wash. In a saucepan with salted water, simmer bok choy until cooked. Drain; reserve and keep warm. In another saucepan, bring salted water to boil; add noodles and cook 2 to 3 minutes. Remove from heat, cover and let stand until soft; strain before serving.

Heat peanut oil in a skillet; add lobster and chili and toss until heated through. Drizzle lime over lobster and sprinkle with cilantro. Toss to combine.

To serve: In centre of large soup bowls, place bok choy, twist noodles over bok choy and top with lobster mixture. Pour soup around, garnish with additional cilantro and accompany with extra slices of lime.

Serves 4 to 6

*Kaffir lime leaves are found in Asian markets.

HURON COUNTY LOBSTER CHOWDER

Little Inn of Bayfield, Bayfield, ON

Huron County, Ontario, is famous for its beans, which are exported worldwide. The chefs at the Little Inn of Bayfield use a variety of these local beans in their chowder recipe. We have tested the recipe using commercial pre-cooked beans. If you are fortunate enough to obtain fresh, local beans, pre-cook them in advance and add to the recipe, as directed.

2 qt (2 L) water
2 cups (500 mL) sauvignon blanc wine
1 fennel, bulb diced, stalks sliced and leaves minced
2 dozen clams in shell
1 whole lobster, at least 2 lb (1 kg)
4 oz (125 g) bacon, diced
1 onion, diced
2 shallots, chopped
1 large carrot, peeled and diced
2 medium potatoes, peeled and cubed
14-oz (430-mL) can diced plum tomatoes
½ tsp (2 mL) each thyme and marjoram
¼ tsp (1 mL) cayenne pepper
salt and pepper, to taste
2 garlic cloves, minced
1½ cups (375 mL) cooked beans of choice (pinto, kidney, cannellini, etc.)
¼ cup (60 mL) chopped parsley
2 tbsp (30 mL) anise-flavoured liqueur (Pernod, anisette, etc.)

In a stockpot, bring water, wine and chopped fennel stalks to a boil. Add clams and cook until they open, about 5 minutes. Remove clams with a slotted spoon. When cool, remove clam meat and slice in strips; reserve.

Add lobster to stockpot and bring back to a boil; lower heat to medium and cook 12 to 15 minutes. Remove lobster and cool under cold water. When cool enough to handle, break apart and remove meat. Discard stomach sac. Cut meat in chunks and reserve. Lightly crush shells; return to stockpot and bring to a simmer.

In a skillet, sauté bacon until browned; add onion and shallot and sauté until translucent. Add carrot, diced fennel bulb and potato; cook 10 minutes, stirring frequently. Add tomatoes, thyme, marjoram, cayenne, salt, pepper, garlic and beans; stir to combine.

Strain stock and return to stockpot; add bacon and vegetable mixture and simmer 30 to 40 minutes. Add clams, lobster, parsley, chopped fennel leaves and liqueur; bring to serving temperature and adjust seasoning. Serve with bread of choice.

Serves 6

LOBSTER BISQUE

C Restaurant, Vancouver, BC

Creative chefs love to introduce personal ingredients to traditional recipes. The kitchen at C Restaurant enhances the delicate lobster flavour of their bisque with a subtle infusion of exotic spices — the results are spectacular!

2 lb (1 kg) cooked lobster bodies and claw shells
½ cup (125 mL) butter
1 small carrot, chopped
1 small stalk celery, chopped
1 red pepper, chopped
1 red onion, chopped
1 head fennel, chopped
1 tomato, chopped
5 garlic cloves, minced
4 bay leaves
4 star anise, toasted*
4 whole cloves, toasted*
1 tbsp (15 mL) annatto seed paste** (or a pinch of saffron)
1 tbsp (15 mL) white peppercorns
1 tbsp (15 mL) maple syrup
1 cup (250 mL) white wine
½ cup (125 mL) brandy
8 cups (2 L) heavy cream (35% M.F.)

Remove the lobsters' sand sacs (the organ located behind the eyes); break up lobster bodies and claws into medium-sized pieces. Reserve.

Heat butter in a large saucepan over medium-low heat. Add vegetables and spices and sweat, covered, until vegetables are softened and begin to colour, about 5 minutes. Add lobster shells and maple syrup and cook, uncovered, until they begin to stick and there is no moisture, about 8 minutes. Raise heat to medium-high, add wine and brandy and deglaze, stirring frequently, until liquid evaporates.

Reduce heat to medium, add cream and slowly bring to a simmer, being careful not to boil. Remove from heat, cool to room temperature and then refrigerate for 2 hours, allowing flavours to blend. Bring back to room temperature and strain through a fine-mesh strainer. Return bisque to saucepan, bring back to a low simmer and cook for 2 minutes. Serve immediately.

Serves 6

*To toast spices: heat a heavy skillet over medium heat until hot. Add spices and toast, stirring frequently, until fragrant, about 2 to 5 minutes.

**Annatto seed paste is a derivative of the achiote seed and is commonly used in Mexican cookery for its flavour and yellow colouring. It can be found in Mexican food stores.

LUNCH

These lunch and "one-dish" meals are perfect for people with busy lifestyles. Seafood Crèpes with Lemon Caper Sauce and Fresh Atlantic Lobster Soufflé, served with a salad, are excellent choices for a light dinner.

LOBSTER RAVIOLI IN LEMON CREAM

Step'n Out Eclectic Cuisine, Winnipeg, MB

Rich, yet delicately flavourful, this luncheon dish will delight your palate and bring accolades from your guests.

2 eggs
1 tbsp (15 mL) finely minced onion
1 tbsp (15 mL) finely minced garlic
10 oz (300 g) lobster meat, chopped
⅓ cup (75 mL) chopped fresh parsley
⅓ cup (75 mL) chopped fresh basil
zest of 2 lemons
½ cup (125 mL) breadcrumbs
1 tsp (5 mL) honey
salt and pepper
12 oz (1 pkg) gyoza (dumpling) wrappers
egg wash (1 beaten egg + ½ tsp/2 mL water)
Cream Sauce (recipe follows)
Gremolata (recipe follows)
1 pkg (375 g) fresh spinach

In a medium-sized bowl, whisk eggs. Add onion, garlic, lobster, parsley, basil, lemon zest, breadcrumbs, honey, salt and pepper; mix to combine. Mixture should be firm; add additional breadcrumbs, if necessary.

If using a dough press, place wrapper on press, brush edges with egg wash and place 1 tbsp (15 mL) lobster mixture in centre of wrapper. Fold dough press to form a furled crescent shape. If shaping by hand, place wrapper on work surface, brush edges with egg wash and centre 1 tbsp (15 mL) lobster mixture. Fold in half, forming a crescent shape, and crimp firmly to seal. Place ravioli on baking sheet covered with a damp towel. Repeat process with the rest of the mixture.

In a large saucepan two-thirds full of boiling salted water, cook 4 to 5 ravioli at a time until they rise to the top and are cooked, about 4 minutes. With a slotted spoon, remove ravioli to an oiled baking sheet and cool. Repeat until all are cooked.

Add ravioli to warm Cream Sauce and bring to serving temperature. In a saucepan of boiling water, cook spinach until wilted, about 1 minute; drain well.

To serve: centre spinach on 6 warmed serving plates; top with ravioli and spoon additional Cream Sauce around. Garnish with sprinkling of Gremolata.

Serves 6

CREAM SAUCE

1 tsp (5 mL) olive oil
2 tbsp (30 mL) minced onion
2 tbsp (30 mL) roasted garlic,* minced
½ cup (125 mL) white wine
2 tbsp (30 mL) butter, cubed
juice of 2 lemons
2 cups (500 mL) heavy cream (35% M.F.)
salt and pepper

In a skillet, heat olive oil; add onion and cook until translucent. Stir in roasted garlic and deglaze pan with wine. Whisk in butter, lemon juice and cream; cook on low heat for flavours to fuse, about 10 minutes. Remove from heat, cover and let rest another 10 minutes. Strain through a fine sieve and return to skillet; adjust seasoning with salt and pepper to taste.

GREMOLATA (GARNISH)

2 tbsp (30 mL) chopped fresh basil
2 tbsp (30 mL) chopped fresh parsley
zest of 1 lemon

In a bowl, toss together basil, parsley and lemon zest.

*To roast garlic: Remove outer skin from whole garlic bulbs and trim ½ inch (1 cm) from the pointed end. Pour a small amount of olive oil over the cut ends and bake, covered, in preheated 375°F (190°C) oven until cloves are browned and soft, about 30 minutes. Squeeze individual cloves from bulb. Store refrigerated 3 to 4 days or freeze.

LOBSTER CLUB SANDWICH

The ultimate lobster sandwich — served Maritime-style with a side of coleslaw and fries!

3 slices of white bread, toasted
mayonnaise
shredded lettuce
thin tomato slices
3 strips bacon, cooked crisp and drained
4 oz (125 g) lobster meat

Spread first slice of toast with mayonnaise and cover with lettuce, tomato, and bacon. Cover with second slice of toast, spread with mayonnaise and lobster meat. Spread mayonnaise on one side of the third slice of toast and place on top of the sandwich. To serve, cut in quarters and secure with toothpicks. Garnish as desired.

Serves 1

LOBSTER CAESAR SALAD

1 head of fresh romaine, trimmed
Caesar Dressing (recipe follows)
¼ cup parmesan, shredded
meat from 1 lobster, ½ lb (250 g)
fresh bread croutons
6 strips of bacon, chopped and cooked crispy

Trim and wash the romaine heads. Gently dry the romaine in a salad spinner. In a large bowl, mix together the Caesar dressing, romaine, and half of the parmesan. Combine well and portion onto 2 plates. The lobster can be served cold or gently warmed up in a pan butter. Top the salad with extra parmesan, croutons, bacon lardons and lobster.

CAESAR DRESSING

2 large egg yolks
1 tbsp Dijon mustard
1 tsp minced garlic
2 anchovies, minced
juice of 1 lemon
¾ cup olive oil
salt and pepper to taste
few drops Worcestershire sauce
few drops tabasco sauce

To prepare the Caesar dressing, add the yolks into a large bowl or food processor. Combine the yolks with the mustard, garlic, anchovies and lemon juice. While whisking (or with the food processor on), begin to slowly add the olive oil to emulsify the dressing. Once all the oil has been added finish with the salt, pepper, Worcestershire sauce and tabasco.

Serves 2

LOBSTER ROLL

Mountain Gap Inn, Smith's Cove, NS

The traditional lobster roll is served across the Maritime Provinces accompanied by coleslaw and fries. We tested the sandwich using a roll recipe from The Compass Rose, Grand Manan Island.

3 cups (750 mL) cooked lobster meat, in bite-sized pieces
¼ cup (60 mL) celery, chopped fine
mayonnaise
salt and pepper to taste
4 "Lobster" Rolls (recipe follows)
shredded lettuce

Fold together lobster and celery with just enough mayonnaise to bind them. Season with salt and pepper. Split four rolls almost through and toast lightly. Place lettuce on rolls and fill with lobster mixture.

Serves 4

"LOBSTER" ROLLS

1 tbsp (15 mL) dry yeast
1 tsp (5 mL) granulated sugar
½ cup (125 mL) lukewarm water
⅓ cup (75 mL) granulated sugar (2nd amount)
1 tsp (5 mL) salt
⅓ cup (75 mL) oil
1⅔ cups (400 mL) warm water
5–6 cups (1.3–1.5 L) all-purpose flour
1 tbsp (15 mL) butter

Dissolve yeast and 1 teaspoon (5 mL) sugar in lukewarm water and let rise to at least 1 cup (250 mL) in volume. Combine sugar (2nd amount), salt, oil and warm water in a large bowl and whisk briskly. Add yeast mixture to other liquids and beat until smooth. Gradually add flour, a cupful at a time, beating after each addition, until you need to use your hands to combine the remainder.

Turn out on a flour-covered surface and knead until smooth and slightly sticky, about 5 minutes. Place dough in a greased bowl and turn to cover with oil. Cover and let rise for 45 minutes in a warm, draft-free place.

Punch down and shape into 12 oblong rolls. Place on a greased baking sheet, cover loosely and let rise again for 45 minutes.

Preheat oven to 375°F (190°C). Bake rolls for 12 to 15 minutes, until slightly golden. Remove from oven, brush tops with butter and cool on wire racks.

Yields 12 "lobster" rolls

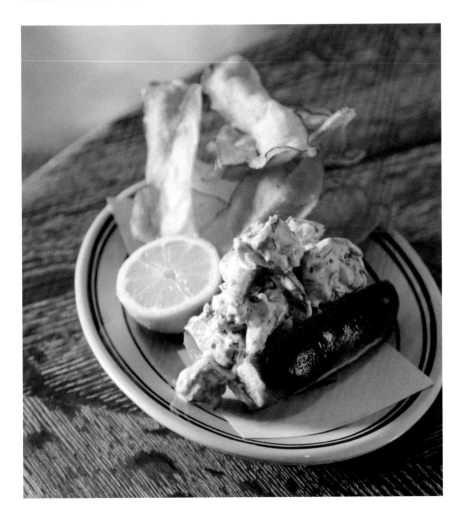

LOBSTER ON POTATO PANCAKES WITH SOUR CREAM SAUCE

Dufferin Inn and San Martello Dining Room
Saint John, NB

Owner/Chef Axel Begner brings a German flavour to Atlantic lobster when he serves it on potato pancakes accompanied by a sour cream sauce.

3 medium-sized potatoes, peeled
1 tbsp (15 mL) all-purpose flour
1 egg, slightly beaten
vegetable oil for frying
1½ cups (375 mL) fresh lobster meat, cooked
Sour Cream Sauce (recipe follows)

Grate potatoes into a large bowl. Stir in flour and beaten egg. Heat a skillet and brush with a small amount of oil. Drop heaping tablespoons of potato mixture onto hot skillet and fry pancakes until golden brown on one side. Flip pancakes, press with a spatula to flatten, and fry until golden. Remove from skillet, set on paper towels to remove any excess oil and keep warm.

To serve, arrange pancakes on individual plates, top with lobster and nap with Sour Cream Sauce.

Serves 4 to 6

SOUR CREAM SAUCE

½ cup (125 mL) sour cream
½ tsp (2 mL) prepared horseradish
½ tsp (2 mL) lemon juice
pinch of sugar
1 green onion, thinly sliced
salt and pepper to taste

Combine all ingredients in a small bowl and whisk until blended. Refrigerate.

LOBSTER TOAST POINTS

Inn on the Lake, Fall River, NS

At the inn, this dish is served with fresh parsley and a side salad. It provides an ample luncheon serving or light dinner entrée.

¼ lb (125 g) fresh mushrooms, diced
8–12 oz (225–375 g) cooked lobster meat, in bite-sized chunks
3 tbsp (45 mL) grated carrot
2½ tbsp (35 mL) fish stock
½ tsp (2 mL) sweet Hungarian paprika (or to taste)
1 cup (250 mL) heavy cream (35% M.F.)
¼ lb (125 g) cheddar cheese, grated
4 thick slices white bread
8 sprigs fresh parsley, chopped

Combine mushrooms, lobster, carrot, stock, paprika and cream in a large saucepan and cook over medium heat until slightly thickened. Add cheese and stir until melted. Toast bread and cut in wedges. Serve lobster mixture spooned over toast and garnished with fresh parsley.

Serves 4

SEAFOOD CRÈPES WITH LEMON CAPER SAUCE

This impressive luncheon dish is both inexpensive and easy to prepare. We found that the lemon caper sauce is delicious served with other seafood as well.

2 tbsp (30 mL) butter
1 tbsp (15 mL) vegetable oil
1 small onion, diced
1 small green pepper, diced
1 garlic clove, crushed
4 oz (125 g) cooked lobster, chopped
8 oz (225 g) crab meat
1 tbsp (15 mL) brandy (optional)
salt and freshly ground pepper to taste
Basic Crèpes to serve 4 (recipe follows)
Lemon Caper Sauce (recipe follows)

Heat butter and oil in a skillet; add onion, green pepper and garlic and sauté until vegetables are softened but not browned. Add lobster and crab meat and cook for 1 minute; stir in brandy. Remove from heat, add salt and pepper to taste and reserve.

Preheat oven to 350°F (180°C). To assemble: divide seafood filling among crèpes and roll up, enclosing the ends. Place seam side down in a greased shallow baking dish, cover with foil and bake for 15 minutes. Serve with warm Lemon Caper Sauce.

Serves 4

BASIC CRÈPE RECIPE

The crèpes may be made in advance. Separate them with waxed paper, wrap them tightly in foil and freeze. To thaw, simply remove quantity needed and bring to room temperature.

2 eggs
1 cup (250 mL) milk
¾ cup (175 mL) all-purpose flour
pinch of salt

Whisk together eggs and milk. Add flour and salt and continue beating until the batter is smooth. Rest batter for 1 hour.

Brush a non-stick skillet with a little vegetable oil and heat on medium. Add enough batter to barely cover the bottom of the pan (scant ¼ cup/50 mL) and cook for approximately 30 seconds. Flip crèpe and cook for another 15 seconds. Repeat, setting crèpes aside to cool.

Makes approximately 1 dozen large or 16 medium crèpes

LEMON CAPER SAUCE

1 cup (250 mL) chicken broth
⅓ cup (75 mL) butter
3 tbsp (45 mL) fresh lemon juice
1 egg yolk, beaten
1 tbsp (15 mL) water
2 tsp (10 mL) cornstarch
1 tbsp (15 mL) capers, drained and chopped
white pepper to taste

Bring broth, butter and lemon juice to a boil over medium-high heat, stirring until the butter melts. Reduce heat to low. Blend egg, water and cornstarch until creamy. Stir small amount of hot mixture into egg, add to hot mixture and cook, stirring constantly until thickened. Do not boil. Remove from heat, stir in capers and season to taste with pepper. Serve warm.

FRESH ATLANTIC LOBSTER SOUFFLÉ

Accompany this soufflé with assorted greens dressed with fresh herb vinaigrette. Always serve a soufflé straight from the oven when it is puffed and airy.

16 cups (4 L) water
1 tbsp (15 mL) salt
1 medium onion, peeled and halved
1 medium carrot, peeled and diced
2 stalks celery
2 small bay leaves
4 whole cloves
6 whole allspice
2–3 tomatoes, cut in chunks
1 tbsp (15 mL) paprika
1½ lb (650 g) lobster
2 tbsp (30 mL) unsalted butter
2 tbsp (30 mL) all-purpose flour
¼ cup (60 mL) heavy cream (35% M.F.), warmed
1 cup (250 mL) reserved lobster stock
¼ tsp (1 mL) lemon juice
1 tbsp (15 mL) brandy
6 whole eggs, separated
salt and freshly ground white pepper to taste

Pour water into large stockpot. Add salt, onion, carrot, celery, bay leaves, cloves, allspice, tomatoes and paprika. Bring to a boil; reduce heat and simmer 15 minutes. Return to full boil, add lobster, cover and cook 15 minutes. Remove lobster from pot and set aside to cool. Keep stock hot.

Twist the tail and claws from the lobster body. Remove meat from shells, cut into small chunks and reserve. Split body in half, place in stockpot and return to a boil. Reduce heat and simmer 1 hour. Strain, discarding solids and reserving stock.

Preheat oven to 400°F (200°C). In a heavy saucepan, melt butter and whisk in flour. Cook over low heat for 1 minute, then add cream and 1 cup (250 mL) reserved lobster stock. Bring to a boil, whisking constantly until sauce thickens. Remove from heat; whisk in lemon juice, brandy and egg yolks. Add lobster meat, season with salt and pepper and set aside.

Butter and lightly flour a 2-quart (2-L) soufflé dish. Beat egg whites until stiff, but not dry, then gently fold in the lobster mixture. Pour into soufflé dish and bake for 15 to 20 minutes, until puffed and browned. Serve immediately.

Serves 4

LOBSTER AND PASTA

The addition of lime gives a most delightful flavour to this dish! We served it on a bed of fresh fettucini.

1 tbsp (15 mL) olive oil
2–3 garlic cloves, minced
12 oz (375 g) lobster meat, in bite-sized pieces
1 tbsp (15 mL) fresh basil, chopped (or 1 tsp/5 mL dried)
1 tbsp (15 mL) fresh chives, chopped (or 1 tsp/5 mL dried)
1 tbsp (15 mL) fresh oregano (or 1 tsp/5 mL dried)
2–3 fresh tomatoes, cut in wedges
19-oz (540-mL) can Italian-style plum tomatoes
zest and juice of 1 lime
salt and pepper to taste
¼ cup (60 mL) freshly grated Parmesan cheese
pasta of choice to serve 4

Heat olive oil in a heavy-bottomed saucepan, add garlic and sauté until softened, being careful not to brown. Stir in lobster and sauté until heated through. Add herbs, fresh and canned tomatoes, lime juice and zest. Season with salt and pepper. Stir in Parmesan cheese and return to serving temperature.

Cook pasta until al dente. Drain and serve topped with sauce and garnished with fresh herbs and additional Parmesan cheese, if desired.

Serves 4

LOBSTER IN VANILLA CREAM SAUCE

Edgewater Manor Restaurant, Stoney Creek, ON

At Edgewater Manor Restaurant, the chef uses a vanilla bean to infuse the flavour of this cream sauce. He simmers the bean in the cream mixture for 5 minutes, then splits it and scrapes the seeds into the sauce, removing the pod. For the ease of the home cook, we offer simpler directions using pure vanilla extract.

2 tbsp (30 mL) butter
2 tbsp (30 mL) chopped shallots
¼ cup (60 mL) dry white wine
2 cups (500 mL) heavy cream (35% M.F.)
1 tsp (5 mL) pure vanilla extract
1 lb (450 g) cooked lobster tails and claws, shelled and drained
salt and pepper
4 pre-baked puff pastry cups

Melt butter over medium heat and sauté shallots until transparent. Deglaze the pan with wine and reduce by half. Stir in cream and vanilla and bring to a boil. Reduce heat and simmer until sauce has reduced by half and thickened slightly. Stir in lobster pieces and season with salt and pepper. Serve in puff pastry cups.

Serves 4

MAINS

Behold, an array of dishes suitable for family gatherings or gala entertaining! From Dalvay by the Sea's Barbecued Lobster with Red Pepper and Lime Butter to Lobster Mac & Cheese, there is something for everyone's taste.

BARBECUED LOBSTER WITH RED PEPPER AND LIME BUTTER

Dalvay by the Sea, Dalvay, PEI

This lobster recipe, with its subtle roasted red pepper and lime, provides a completely different flavour from boiled lobster. Complete your feast with an accompaniment of spicy Jamaican Coleslaw!

4 lobsters, 1–1½ lb (450–650 g) each
1 red bell pepper
2 tbsp (30 mL) oil
1 cup (250 mL) butter, softened
juice and zest of 2 limes
salt and pepper to taste
pinch of cayenne pepper
½ cup (125 mL) olive oil
2 garlic cloves, chopped
juice of 1 lemon
½ cup (125 mL) chopped chives
½ cup (125mL) chopped cilantro
coarsely ground black pepper
lemon wedges, as garnish

Bring a large pot of salted water to a boil; plunge lobsters in for 4 to 6 minutes to blanch. Remove lobsters and cool until you can handle them. Cut in half lengthwise, remove viscera, and crack claws.

Preheat oven to 425°F (220°C). Brush red pepper with oil, place on a baking sheet and roast for 15 minutes, turning several times. Remove from oven and cool. Carefully peel off pepper skin, remove seeds and chop the pepper. Place softened butter, red pepper, lime juice and zest in a blender and process until smooth. Season with salt, pepper and cayenne. Set aside at room temperature.

Prepare marinade by combining olive oil, garlic, lemon juice, chives, cilantro and black pepper. Rub thoroughly over lobster and let stand for 20 minutes. Barbecue lobster flesh-side down on a hot grill until golden. Turn, brush flesh with red pepper butter and cook, shell-side down for another

6 to 8 minutes, allowing the lobster to braise in its own juices. Arrange lobster on warm plates, top with remaining red pepper butter and serve with a large spoonful of Jamaican Coleslaw (recipe follows) and a garnish of lemon wedges.

JAMAICAN COLESLAW

¼ head red cabbage
¼ head chinese cabbage
1 red onion
2 stalks celery
1 large carrot
1 garlic clove, minced
½ tsp (2 mL) ground cumin
½ tsp (2 mL) ground coriander seeds
½ tsp (2 mL) curry powder
½ tsp (2 mL) Dijon mustard
juice of 2 limes
¼ cup (50 mL) red wine vinegar
1 cup (250 mL) olive oil
salt and pepper to taste

Thinly slice the cabbage and onion and cut the celery and carrot in thin julienne matchsticks. Set aside in a large bowl. Place remaining ingredients, except salt and pepper, in a blender and process. Pour sauce over vegetables and mix well. Season with salt and pepper.

Serves 4

FRESH STEAMED LOBSTER

This failproof recipe for freshly steamed lobster was given to us by innkeepers in Lunenburg, NS. We suggest you remove the rubber bands from the lobster claws before cooking, as they transfer a rubber taste to the lobster meat.

2 lobsters, 1 lb (450 g) each
romaine leaves, as garnish
½ cup (125 mL) melted butter
1 lemon, sliced in wedges
parsley sprigs, as garnish

Use a steamer pot or place a vegetable steamer in an appropriately sized pot with enough water to cover the bottom of the steamer by 1 inch (2.5 cm). Bring the water to a hard boil, place lobsters in the steamer and cover. Cooking time will vary depending on the size of the lobsters, but a 1-lb (450-g) lobster is cooked in 15 minutes.

When cooked, remove the lobster from the pot and briefly cool under cold water. For ease of eating, crack the lobster in the kitchen: place the lobster upside down; take a cleaver and place the point at the beginning of the tail; slice down the middle, breaking right through the outer shell. With the lobster still on its back, bring the cleaver sharply down on each claw and twist sideways, forcing the claw shell apart.

For presentation, put two romaine leaves on a plate and place the lobster on top, with the front covering the stems of the romaine. Between the claws place a small bowl of melted butter. Position two lemon wedges where the claws join the body and parsley sprigs between the lemons and along the cut made in the tail. Take a paper towel dipped in a small amount of the melted butter and rub over the lobster shell. Bon appetit!

Serves 2

LOBSTER ORIENTAL

Well-known New Brunswick chef and restaurateur couple Ross and Willa Mavis shared this recipe with us a number of years ago. To give the dish a local flavour, they like to use blanched fiddleheads instead of broccoli or zucchini. Try it with your own choice of in-season vegetable combinations.

2 cups (500 mL) lobster meat
2 tbsp (30 mL) canola oil
1 cup (250 mL) fresh mushrooms, sliced
1 cup (250 mL) celery, diagonally sliced
1 cup (250 mL) cauliflower florets
1 cup (250 mL) broccoli florets or sliced zucchini
1 red or yellow pepper, cubed
½ cup (125 mL) fish or chicken stock
1 tbsp (15 mL) cornstarch
1 tbsp (15 mL) cold water
1 tbsp (15 mL) soya or oyster sauce
⅛ tsp (½ mL) hot red pepper flakes, or to taste
salt and pepper to taste
1 tsp (5 mL) dulse flakes (optional)

Coarsely chop lobster, removing cartilage and any shell pieces; set aside. In a wok or large skillet, heat canola oil over medium-high heat. Add vegetables and stir or toss quickly for 1 to 2 minutes. Add stock and cover to allow vegetables to steam until crisp tender. Mix cornstarch with cold water; add soya or oyster sauce and hot pepper flakes. Stir into hot broth in wok and coat all vegetables. Add lobster and heat through. Add salt and pepper to season, then sprinkle with dulse flakes and serve with rice or pasta.

Serves 4

ASTICE CON FUNGHI (LOBSTER WITH WILD MUSHROOMS)

Da Maurizio, Halifax, NS

The addition of wild portobello and porcini mushrooms gives this Northern Italian entrée a delicate woodsy flavour.

1 oz (30 g) dried porcini mushrooms
½ cup (125 mL) white wine
4 lobsters, 1½ lb (650 g) each
Cooking Stock (recipe follows)
¼ cup (60 mL) butter
1 small onion, diced
12 oz (375 g) fresh portobello mushrooms, stems removed
2 cups (500 mL) tomato sauce
6 fresh basil leaves (or ¼ tsp/1 mL dried)
salt and pepper to taste

Soak porcini mushrooms in white wine and let stand for 30 minutes.

Prepare lobsters according to Cooking Stock directions (see below). Carefully remove meat from claws and tails; keep warm.

In a large skillet, melt butter, add onion and sauté until translucent. Slice portobello mushrooms ¼-inch (½-cm) thick and add to onions. Sauté until tender, approximately 5 minutes. Add porcini mushrooms, wine, tomato sauce and basil, cooking until sauce is reduced and slightly thickened. Season with salt and pepper.

To serve, spoon sauce onto four plates and arrange lobster on top in its original shape.

Serves 4

COOKING STOCK

8 cups (2 L) water
4 tbsp (60 mL) coarse salt
1 medium onion, quartered
1 stalk celery, chopped
1 medium carrot, chopped
2 bay leaves
1 sprig parsley
1 sprig thyme
1 lemon, quartered

In a large stockpot, combine all ingredients. Bring to a boil, reduce heat and simmer for 15 minutes. Return to a hard boil, plunge lobsters into water and bring back to a boil. Reduce heat and cook lobsters for 16 minutes. Remove lobsters and cool to room temperature.

LOBSTER TRUFFLE GNOCCHI WITH LOBSTER EMULSION

Diva at the Met, Vancouver, BC

Truffle oil with its earthy essence has a very concentrated flavour and should be used in moderation. This is one instance where "a little is heavenly" and "more is not better." You will find truffle oil in specialty food markets.

2 live lobsters, 1½ lb (650 g) each
4 tbsp (60 mL) butter, divided
⅓ cup (75 mL) diced celeriac
¼ cup (60 mL) chicken stock
1 tsp (5 mL) white truffle oil
Gnocchi (recipe follows)
Lobster Emulsion (recipe follows)
white truffles, as garnish (optional)

Bring a large pot of water to a boil. Add lobsters, bring back to a boil and cook for 2 minutes. Remove lobsters; pull off tails and claws, reserving tails for another use. Return claws to boiling water and cook for 5 minutes longer. Lift claws from water and, while warm, remove shells with scissors, keeping the claw meat in one piece. Reserve and refrigerate claw meat. Cut lobster bodies in half; discard eyes and stomach sac and rinse well under water to clean. Break shells and bodies into smaller pieces and reserve for emulsion.

Prepare Gnocchi and Lobster Emulsion.

Place lobster claw meat on a small baking sheet and brush with 1 tbsp (15 mL) softened butter. Place in preheated 350°F (180°C) oven for 5 minutes to warm. In a skillet, heat 1 tbsp (15 mL) butter, add celeriac and sauté until soft, about 4 minutes. Add reserved Gnocchi, chicken stock and remaining butter. Simmer until stock has slightly thickened and coats Gnocchi. Add truffle oil and adjust seasoning.

To serve: divide Gnocchi among 4 plates; top Gnocchi with a lobster claw that has been sliced on the diagonal. Whisk the Lobster Emulsion to create a froth and gently spoon around Gnocchi. If using truffles, shave slices on top to garnish plates.

GNOCCHI

2 medium russet potatoes
½–¾ cup (125–175 mL) all-purpose flour
2 egg yolks, beaten
1 tsp (5 mL) salt
olive oil

Bake potatoes in a preheated 375°F (190°C) oven for 1 hour or until completely cooked. Peel potatoes while still warm, and mash or press through a ricer. Place warm potatoes in a bowl and make a well in the centre. To the well, add ½ cup (125 mL) flour, egg yolks and salt; gently fold with a wooden spoon until ingredients are incorporated and the mixture is not sticky. Use additional flour if the potato mixture is on the wet side. Roll the dough into a ball and portion into three pieces.

On a floured work-surface, roll each piece of dough into ⅛-inch (¼-cm) strips and cut into ½-inch (1-cm) pieces. Drop pieces into a large pot of boiling water and cook until the gnocchi float to the top. Remove gnocchi with a slotted spoon, place on a baking sheet and drizzle with olive oil. Cool and reserve.

LOBSTER EMULSION

2 tomatoes, chopped
⅓ cup (75 mL) diced carrot
1½ tbsp (20 mL) fresh tarragon
2 cups (500 mL) heavy cream (35% M.F.)

In a saucepan over medium-high heat, add lobster bodies and sauté for 2 minutes; add tomatoes, carrots and tarragon and sauté for an additional 2 minutes. Add enough water to cover shells and simmer on low heat for 1 hour. Strain stock through a fine-mesh strainer into a small saucepan. Return stock to simmer and reduce to 1 cup. Add cream and simmer until reduced to 2 cups. Keep warm.

Serves 4

LOBSTER AND CHICKEN SUPREME

Marshlands Inn, Sackville, NB

The chefs at Marshlands Inn cut the chicken and lobster pieces in medallions and serve them alternately on the plate. Drizzled with a rich sherry-flavoured cream sauce, this dish is a perfect entrée for special occasions.

2 lobsters, 1½ lb (650 g) each
5 tbsp (75mL) vegetable oil, portioned
½ cup (125 mL) sherry
1⅓ cups (325 mL) heavy cream (35% M.F.)
4 boneless chicken breasts, 4 oz (125 g) each
flour, for dusting
salt and pepper to taste

Bring a large kettle of salted water to a full boil. Plunge lobsters head first into water and hold under water with a wooden spoon for 4 minutes. Remove from water and set aside until cool enough to handle.

Separate claws and tails from lobster bodies. Remove tomalley from bodies and reserve. (Tomalley is the soft olive-green liver, found in the body of the lobster. It is considered a delicacy, and can be eaten alone or incorporated into sauces.)

Crack claws and slice tails (shells and meat) into medallions. In a large skillet, heat 3 tbsp (45 mL) oil until hot and sauté lobster pieces, stirring occasionally, for 2 to 3 minutes. Deglaze pan with sherry, bring to a boil; add cream and simmer for 8 to 10 minutes until cooked.

Preheat oven to 400°F (200°C). Dredge chicken in flour, coating lightly. Heat 2 tbsp (30 mL) oil over high heat in a heavy ovenproof skillet and brown chicken, turning once. Place skillet in oven and bake until chicken is no longer pink in the centre (5 to 7 minutes).

With a slotted spoon, remove lobster from pan. Separate meat from shells and keep warm. Return sauce to medium heat, whisk in reserved tomalley and juices and reduce until slightly thickened. Season sauce with salt and pepper. Arrange lobster and chicken on plates and top with cream sauce.

Serves 4

LOBSTER MAC & CHEESE

A new take on an old favourite.

1lb (450 g) elbow macaroni
olive oil
4 cups (1 L) milk
8 tbsp (120 mL) unsalted butter, divided
1 small onion, diced
3 cloves of garlic, minced
½ tsp (2 mL) fennel seeds
2 bay leaves
½ cup (125 g) all-purpose flour
1 cup (250 g) Gruyere cheese, grated
1 cup (250 g) sharp Cheddar, grated
½ tsp (2 mL) kosher salt
½ tsp (2 mL) ground black pepper
1 bunch parsley, chopped
1 lb (450 g) cooked lobster meat, cut into small chunks (meat from 2 lobsters)
1½ cups (375 mL) panko breadcrumbs

Preheat the oven to 375°F (180°C)

Bring a large pot of salted water to a boil. Add the pasta and cook according to the directions on the package. Drain well and coat with a small amount of olive oil to prevent sticking. Heat the milk in a saucepan. In a large pot, melt 6 tablespoons of the butter and gently cook onions, garlic, fennel and bay leaves until aromatic but not coloured. Add in the flour. Cook over low heat for 1 minute, constantly stirring. Still stirring, add the hot milk gradually and cook for a minute or two more, until thickened and smooth. Take off the heat, add the cheeses, salt and pepper. Add the cooked macaroni, parsley and lobster and stir well. Place the mixture in 6 individual gratin dishes, or one large casserole dish. Melt the remaining butter and combine with the fresh breadcrumbs; sprinkle on the top of the dishes. Bake for 30 to 35 minutes for the individual gratins, or 45 to 60 minutes for the casserole, or until golden brown and bubbling hot.

Serves 4 to 6

LOBSTER NEWBURG

Amherst Shore Country Inn, Lorneville, NS

At the Amherst Shore Country Inn, the first person of the day to make a dinner reservation might be asked by the innkeeper to decide the menu for that evening. This entrée is often requested.

⅓ cup (75 mL) butter
4 cups (1 L) fresh lobster meat, in bite-sized pieces
generous dash of paprika
generous dash of nutmeg
½ cup (125 mL) medium-dry sherry
6 egg yolks, lightly beaten
2 cups (500 mL) heavy cream (35% M.F.)
6 pre-baked puff pastry shells

Melt butter in the top of a double boiler over hot, but not boiling, water. Add lobster meat and sauté gently until heated through. Add paprika, nutmeg and sherry, and return to serving temperature. Blend egg yolks and cream with a wire whisk; add to the lobster and heat gently until hot and the sauce begins to thicken. Do not boil. Serve immediately in a puff pastry shell, over rice or with a medley of seasonal vegetables.

Serves 6

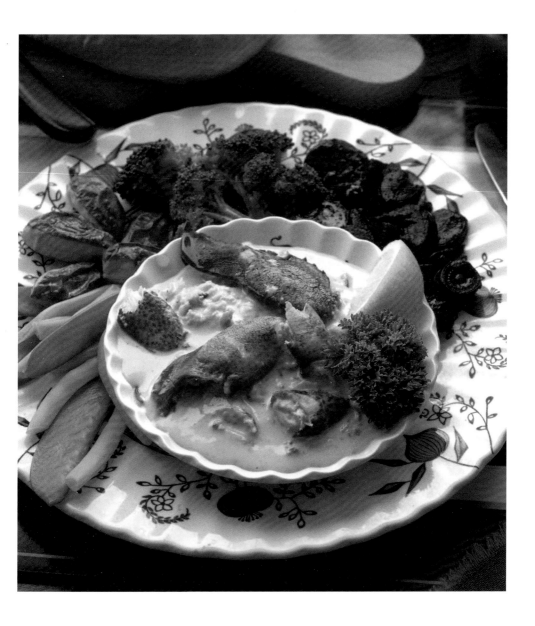

SEAFOOD LASAGNA

The Compass Rose, Grand Manan Island, NB

Guests at Grand Manan's The Compass Rose are treated to spectacular seafood fresh from the docks at North Head. We tested this recipe using light cottage cheese and milk in place of the cream. While the dish was not as rich, we were delighted with the results.

10 lasagna noodles
1½ lb (650 g) mixed seafood (e.g. lobster, scallops, shrimp, crab, salmon, white fish)
1 lb (450 g) fresh spinach
4 eggs
1 lb (450 g) cottage cheese
salt and pepper to taste
⅛ tsp (½ mL) nutmeg
6 tbsp (90 mL) butter
1 onion, chopped
1 garlic clove, crushed
1 tbsp (15 mL) fresh dill
6 tbsp (90 mL) all-purpose flour
salt and pepper to taste
2 tbsp (30 mL) sherry
3 cups (750 mL) light cream (10% M.F.)
1 cup (250 mL) grated Swiss cheese
½ cup (125 mL) grated Parmesan cheese

Cook lasagna noodles until tender and drain and rinse under cold water. Set aside. In boiling salted water, poach raw seafood until barely cooked. Drain and reserve. Briefly blanch spinach, drain well and chop. Lightly beat eggs. In a large bowl, combine eggs, spinach and cottage cheese. Season with salt, pepper and nutmeg. Set aside.

Preheat oven to 350°F (180°C). Melt butter and sauté onion and garlic until soft. Add dill, flour, salt and pepper and cook, stirring constantly, over medium heat for 1 minute. Whisk sherry and cream into flour mixture a little at a time, until smooth and well blended. Cook, stirring constantly, until thickened. Add Swiss cheese and seafood to sauce, stirring until cheese is melted.

To assemble, place half of the noodles in a greased 9" x 13" (22 cm x 33 cm) lasagna pan. Spread half of the spinach mixture over noodles and cover with half of the seafood sauce. Repeat layers and top with grated Parmesan cheese. Bake for 45 minutes to an hour, or until bubbly and lightly browned. Remove from oven and let stand for 10 to 15 minutes before serving.

Serves 6 to 8

LOBSTER IN BENGALI SAUCE WITH MANGO RICE

The chili peppers determine the amount of "heat" in this dish. If a milder sauce is to your liking, use 1 pepper or 1 tsp (5 mL) minced jalapeño pepper (seeds and white membrane removed).

few drops sesame oil
2 tsp (10 mL) vegetable oil
1 medium onion, diced
3 garlic cloves, finely minced
2 tsp (10 mL) grated fresh ginger
2 mild chili peppers, seeded and finely diced (Ancho, Anaheim, Poblano, etc.)
2 cups (500 mL) coconut milk
1 tsp (5 mL) ground coriander
1 tsp (5 mL) turmeric
pinch of cinnamon
1 tsp (5 mL) curry powder
1½ lb (650 g) cooked lobster, in bite-sized chunks
2 tomatoes, diced
salt and pepper
Mango Rice (recipe follows)

Heat sesame oil and vegetable oil over medium heat in a deep frying pan. Sauté onion for 3 minutes, stirring frequently. Add garlic, fresh ginger and chili peppers and continue to cook for 1 minute. Add coconut milk, coriander, turmeric, cinnamon and curry powder and simmer for 10 minutes. Add cooked lobster and diced tomatoes. Cover and let simmer for 2 to 3 minutes. Adjust seasoning with salt and pepper and serve over Mango Rice.

Serves 6

MANGO RICE

1½ cups (375 mL) long grain rice
3 cups (750 mL) chicken stock
3 tbsp (45 mL) butter
1 ripe mango, peeled and diced
½ each red and green bell peppers
1 stalk lemongrass (white part only), peeled and diced
½ cup (125 mL) unsweetened coconut
pinch each of cumin, cardamom, black pepper, salt, ginger, turmeric and curry
  powder

Cook rice in chicken stock according to directions on package. While rice is cooking, melt butter in a skillet and sauté remaining ingredients until peppers are crisp-tender, about 4 minutes. Stir into cooked rice.

CODE DI ARAGOSTA ALLA SUPREMA (LOBSTER TAILS SUPREME)

Da Maurizio, Halifax, NS

If you cannot purchase individual lobster tails, it will be necessary to cook four lobsters weighing 1½ lb (650 g) each, in order to have tails weighing 4–5 oz (125–150 g).

½ cup (125 mL) butter, softened
3 garlic cloves, crushed
3 tbsp (45 mL) parsley, chopped
4 cooked lobster tails, shelled and halved
½ cup (125 mL) white wine
salt and pepper to taste
1 cup (250 mL) heavy cream (35% M.F.)

Blend together butter, garlic and parsley until smooth.

In a skillet over medium-high heat, melt garlic butter. Add lobster tails and sauté for 3 minutes, being careful not to brown butter. Remove lobster with a slotted spoon and reserve. Deglaze pan with wine, season with salt and pepper and reduce liquid by one-half. Add cream and cook until the sauce is thickened. Return lobster to sauce and heat through. Serve immediately with seasonal vegetables of choice.

Serves 4

LOBSTER AND SCALLOPS WITH SUN-DRIED TOMATOES IN BASIL CREAM

Duncreigan Country Inn, Mabou, NS

Sun-dried tomatoes are available either dry or oil-packed. If using the dry variety, reconstitute in warm water to soften, then drain. Always drain tomatoes that are packed in oil.

¾ lb (375 g) large scallops
4 tbsp (60 mL) butter
3–4 shallots, minced
4 cooked lobster tails, split
½ cup (125 mL) white wine
½ cup (125 mL) sun-dried tomatoes, reconstituted (or well-drained, seeded, chopped tomatoes)
4 tbsp (60 mL) fresh basil, chopped
salt and pepper to taste
dash of cayenne
½ cup (125 mL) heavy cream (35% M.F.)
4 oz (125 g) Havarti cheese, grated
fresh pasta to serve 4

Sauté scallops in butter over medium-high heat for 1 minute. Add shallots and lobster tails. Bring to a simmer and cook only until scallops are opaque, about 2 more minutes. Remove from pan and keep warm. Deglaze pan with wine; add tomatoes and basil. Season with salt, pepper and cayenne. Add cream and simmer sauce to thicken slightly. Stir in cheese and heat until melted. Return seafood to sauce and serve immediately over prepared pasta.

Serves 4

EAST COAST MORNAY SAUCE

Vineland Estates Winery Restaurant, Vineland, ON

Ever wonder what to do with the body and legs of your steamed lobster? In this recipe, the chef of Vineland Estates Winery Restaurant shares his secrets, telling us how to make this succulent sauce to serve over white fish or crèpes, or as a dipping sauce. For the photo, we served grilled haddock napped with the sauce.

bodies, legs, and shells of 2–3 lobsters
3 cups (750 mL) heavy cream (35% M.F.)
juice of ½ lemon
1 bay leaf
2 tbsp (30 mL) tomato paste
salt and white pepper
grated Parmesan cheese

Prepare lobster carcasses by reserving any tomalley or roe and discarding stomach, eyes and digestive tract. Crush shells and bodies and place in a heavy saucepan with tomalley, roe, cream, lemon juice and bay leaf. Bring to simmer and cook gently for 50 minutes, stirring occasionally with a wooden spoon. Place a small amount of cream mixture in a bowl and stir in tomato paste. Return to saucepan and simmer for 10 minutes longer.

Strain mixture through a fine sieve, being sure to extract all the juices and tiny bits of lobster meat. Return to a clean saucepan and bring to serving temperature. Adjust seasoning with salt and pepper. Stir in Parmesan cheese, 1 tbsp (15 mL) at a time, until sauce reaches desired thickness.

Yields 1½ cups (375 mL)

BUTTER POACHED LOBSTER

1¾ lb (800 g) live lobster
½ cup (125 mL) salted butter, cut into chunks
2 tbsp (30 mL) shallots, brunoise
4–5 fennel seeds
1 bay leaf

Bring a large pot of water to boil and place in the lobster. Let cook for 3 to 4 minutes. Remove all lobster meat from shell and cut into desired sized pieces (keeping in mind larger pieces will take longer to cook).

In a sauce pan, add a small piece of butter and cook the shallots, fennel and bay leaf gently until aromatic but not coloured. Begin to slowly add in the chunks of butter over low heat, whisking to emulsify as they melt. Make sure the mixture does not come to a boil, otherwise the butter will separate. Add in the lobster pieces while stirring and cook gently over medium-low heat for 6 to 8 minutes (depending on size).

Serve the butter poached lobster on its own with the flavoured butter, add a fresh salad or compliment it with potatoes and fresh vegetables.

Serves 2

INDEX

A

Amherst Shore Country Inn, Lorneville, NS, 80
Astice con Funghi (Lobster with Wild Mushrooms), 72

B

Barbecued Lobster with Red Pepper and Lime Butter, 68
Béarnaise Sauce 16–17
Bisque, Lobster, 44
Butter Poached Lobster, 90

C

C Restaurant, Vancouver, BC, 44
Caesar Dressing, 52
Catch Restaurant, Calgary, AB, 28
chowders
    Dunes' Seafood Chowder with Lobster, 34
    Huron County Lobster Chowder, 42–43
clams
    Huron County Lobster Chowder, 42–43
    Mediterranean Seafood Stew, 28
    Shellfish with Yucatan Flavours, 26
Club Sandwich, Lobster, 50
Code di Aragosta Alla Suprema (Lobster Tails Supreme), 86
Coleslaw, Jamaican, 69
Compass Rose, Grand Manan Island, NB, 54, 82
crab
    Seafood Crèpes with Lemon Caper Sauce, 58
    Seafood Lasagna, 82
Cream Cheese Lobster Cakes, 20
Cream Sauce, 49
Creole Mustard Sauce, 21
Crèpes, Seafood with Lemon Caper Sauce, 58

D

Da Maurizio, Halifax, NS, 72, 86
Dalvay by the Sea, Dalvay, PEI, 68
dips
    Warm Atlantic Lobster Dip, 22
Diva at the Met, Vancouver, BC, 74
Dufferin Inn and San Martello Dining Room, Saint John, NB, 56
Duncreigan Country Inn, Mabou, NS, 87
Dunes Café (The), Brackley Beach, PEI, 34
Dunes' Seafood Chowder with Lobster, 34

E

East Coast Mornay Sauce, 88
Edgewater Manor Restaurant, Stoney Creek, ON, 64

F

Fish Stock, 35
Fresh Atlantic Lobster Soufflé, 60
Fresh Steamed Lobster, 70

G

Gazpacho with Lobster Claws, 36
Gnocchi, 75
Gremolata, 49

H

haddock
    Dunes' Seafood Chowder with Lobster, 34
    Mediterranean Seafood Stew, 28
Hoisin Lobster Lettuce Wraps, 30
Huron County Lobster Chowder, 42–43

I

Inn on the Lake, Fall River, NS, 57

J

Jamaican Coleslaw, 69

L

Lasagna, Seafood, 82

Lemon Caper Sauce, 59
Little Inn of Bayfield, Bayfield, ON, 42
Lobster and Chicken Supreme, 76
Lobster and Pasta, 62
Lobster and Scallops with Sun-dried
  Tomatoes in Basil Cream, 87
Lobster Bisque, 44
Lobster Caesar Salad, 52
Lobster Cakes, Cream Cheese, 20
Lobster Chowder, 42
Lobster Claws, Gazpacho with, 36
Lobster Club Sandwich, 50
Lobster Emulsion, 75
Lobster in Bengali Sauce with Mango
  Rice, 84
Lobster in Vanilla Cream Sauce, 64
Lobster Mac & Cheese, 78
Lobster Newburg, 80
Lobster on Potato Pancakes with Sour
  Cream Sauce, 56
Lobster Oriental, 71
Lobster Potato Salad, 28
Lobster Poutine, 24
Lobster Ravioli in Lemon Cream, 48
Lobster Roll, 54
Lobster Salad, Picant, 27
Lobster Shabu Shabu, 37
Lobster Soufflé, 60
Lobster-Stuffed Tomatoes, 18
Lobster Tails Supreme, 86
Lobster Toast Points, 57
Lobster Truffle Gnocchi with Lobster
  Emulsion, 74
Lobster with Wild Mushrooms, 72
Lobster, Barbecued, with Red Pepper
  and Lime Butter, 68
Lobster, Steamed, 70
Lobster-stuffed Mushroom Caps, 16

M
Mango Rice, 85
Marshlands Inn, Sackville, NB, 76
Mediterranean Seafood Stew, 38
Mornay Sauce, 8
Mountain Gap Inn, Smith's Cove, NS,
  54
Mushroom Caps, Lobster-stuffed, 16
Mushrooms, Wild, with Lobster, 72
mussels

Dunes' Seafood Chowder with
  Lobster, 34
Mediterranean Seafood Stew, 38
Shellfish with Yucatan Flavours, 26
Mustard Sauce, Creole, 21

N
Newburg, Lobster, 80

O
Oriental Lobster, 71

P
pasta
  Lobster Mac & Cheese, 78
  Lobster and Pasta, 62
  Lobster Ravioli in Lemon Cream, 48
  Seafood Lasagna, 82
Pepper Sauce, Sweet, 19
Picant Lobster Salad, 27
Ponzu Sauce, 37
Potato Pancakes with Lobster and Sour
  Cream Sauce, 56
Potato Salad, with Lobster, 28
Poutine, Lobster, 24

R
Ravioli, Lobster in Lemon Cream, 48
Red Pepper and Lime Butter, 68
Rice, Mango, 85
Roll, Lobster, 54

S
salads
  Jamaican Coleslaw, 69
  Lobster Caesar Salad, 52
  Lobster Potato Salad, 28
  Picant Lobster Salad, 27
salmon
  Dunes' Seafood Chowder with
    Lobster, 34
  Seafood Lasagna, 82
Sandwich, Lobster Club, 50
sauces
  Basil Cream, 87
  Bengali Sauce, 84
  Cream Sauce, 49
  Creole Mustard Sauce, 21
  Lemon Caper Sauce, 59
  Lobster Emulsion, 75
  Mornay Sauce, 88

Ponzu Sauce, 37
Red Pepper and Lime Butter, 68
Sour Cream Sauce, 56
Vanilla Cream Sauce, 64
scallops
 Lobster and Scallops with Sun-dried Tomatoes, 87
 Mediterranean Seafood Stew, 28
 Seafood Lasagna, 82
Seafood Chowder with Lobster, 34
Seafood Crèpes with Lemon Caper Sauce, 58
Seafood Lasagna, 82
Seafood Stew, Mediterranean, 38
Shabu Shabu, Lobster, 37
Shellfish with Yucatan Flavours, 26
shrimp
 Dunes' Seafood Chowder with Lobster, 34
 Seafood Lasagna, 82
 Shellfish with Yucatan Flavours, 26
sole
 Dunes' Seafood Chowder with Lobster, 34
Soufflé, Lobster, 60
Sour Cream Sauce, 56
Spicy Thai Lobster Noodle Soup, 40
Steamed Lobster, 70
Step'n Out Eclectic Cuisine, Winnipeg, MB, 48
Stew, Mediterranean Seafood, 38
Stock for lobster, 73
Stock, Fish, 35
Sun-dried Tomatoes, with Lobster and Scallops in Basil Cream, 87
Supreme, Lobster and Chicken, 76
Supreme, Lobster Tails, 86
Sweet Pepper Sauce, 19

T
Thai Lobster Noodle Soup, Spicy, 40
Tomatoes, Lobster-Stuffed, 18

V
Vanilla Cream Sauce, 64
Vineland Estates Winery Restaurant, Vineland, ON, 88

W
Warm Atlantic Lobster Dip, 22

PHOTO CREDITS